Protecting the
OCEANS

PREVENTING OCEAN POLLUTION

By Natalie Hyde

CRABTREE
PUBLISHING COMPANY
WWW.CRABTREEBOOKS.COM

CRABTREE
PUBLISHING COMPANY
WWW.CRABTREEBOOKS.COM

Author: Natalie Hyde

Editorial director: Kathy Middleton

Editor: Janine Deschenes

Proofreader: Wendy Scavuzzo

Design: Margaret Salter

**Production coordinator
and Prepress technician:**
Margaret Salter

Print coordinator: Katherine Berti

Photo Credits:
b=Bottom, l=Left, t=Top, tr=Top Right, tl=Top Left

Fionn Ferreira p13 (tr)

Shutterstock: Bortolomeus Abdi W, p4 (inset);
Rich Carey, p15 (tl); Narongsak Nagadhana, p18
(t); Todor Stoyanov, p26 (l); Wang Junqi, p26 (b);

NOAA's National Centers for Coastal Ocean
Science, p21 (t)

All other images from Shutterstock

Library and Archives Canada Cataloguing in Publication

Title: Preventing ocean pollution / Natalie Hyde.
Names: Hyde, Natalie, 1963- author.
Description: Series statement: Protecting the oceans |
  Includes bibliographical references and index.
Identifiers: Canadiana (print) 20200283758 |
  Canadiana (ebook) 20200283766 |
  ISBN 9780778782018 (hardcover) |
  ISBN 9780778782056 (softcover) |
  ISBN 9781427126054 (HTML)
Subjects: LCSH: Ocean—Juvenile literature. |
  LCSH: Marine pollution—Prevention—Juvenile literature. |
  LCSH: Nature—Effect of human beings on—Juvenile literature.
Classification: LCC GC1090 .H93 2020 | DDC j363.739/47—dc23

Library of Congress Cataloging-in-Publication Data

Names: Hyde, Natalie, 1963- author.
Title: Preventing ocean pollution / Natalie Hyde.
Description: New York : Crabtree Publishing Company, [2021] |
  Series: Protecting the oceans | Includes index.
Identifiers: LCCN 2020029709 (print) | LCCN 2020029710 (ebook) |
  ISBN 9780778782018 (hardcover) |
  ISBN 9780778782056 (paperback) |
  ISBN 9781427126054 (ebook)
Subjects: LCSH: Ocean--Juvenile literature. |
  Marine pollution--Prevention--Juvenile literature.
Classification: LCC GC21.5 .H94 2021 (print) | LCC GC21.5 (ebook) |
  DDC 363.739/47--dc23
LC record available at https://lccn.loc.gov/2020029709
LC ebook record available at https://lccn.loc.gov/2020029710

Crabtree Publishing Company
www.crabtreebooks.com   1-800-387-7650

Printed in the U.S.A./082020/CG20200710

Published in Canada
Crabtree Publishing
616 Welland Ave.
St. Catharines, Ontario
L2M 5V6

Published in the United States
Crabtree Publishing
347 Fifth Ave
Suite 1402-145
New York, NY 10016

Published in the United Kingdom
Crabtree Publishing
Maritime House
Basin Road North, Hove
BN41 1WR

Published in Australia
Crabtree Publishing
3 Charles Street
Coburg North
VIC, 3058

CONTENTS

DROWNING IN PLASTIC

The beach at Muncar, on the island of Java, is drowning in plastic garbage. Plastic from the ocean has washed ashore and sits several feet deep on the beach. Locals have to use an excavator, or digging machine, to dig it out. But new waves just bring more ashore. The plastic wraps around boat propellors, making them unable to turn. Fishermen cannot go out to fish and provide food or an income for their family. Fish stocks are down because plastic sits on feeding grounds. Storm sewers are also clogged, causing more flooding than normal.

Muncar is home to around 130,000 people. It is just one of many cities in Indonesia that is suffering from extreme plastic pollution.

Commercial fishing boats lose or throw away plastic nets, lines, and traps which make up about 10 percent of the plastic waste in the oceans.

Essential Oceans

Our oceans cover 70 percent of Earth's surface. They are home to millions of marine plants and animals. Oceans are also vital to our survival. They give us food, transportation routes, oxygen for our atmosphere, and affect our climate and weather. But we are not taking care of this important resource. Our industries, travel, and waste are causing damage to marine plants and animals and their habitats.

As we realize that polluting our oceans is hurting our own health, changes are slowly starting to happen. Groups and organizations are working hard to make people aware of the dangers and of ways we can change our behavior to protect and **preserve** our oceans.

We dump 17.6 billion pounds (8 billion kg) of plastic into oceans each year about the weight of 57,000 blue whales.

Plastic dumped into the ocean each year

57,000

UNDERSTANDING POLLUTION

Pollution is anything that is introduced into the environment that is unclean, toxic, or causes harm. Chemicals, garbage, and noise are some types of ocean pollution. Noise pollution interferes with the ways many ocean creatures communicate.

Garbage, especially plastic waste, can kill ocean creatures. It can wrap around their bodies, making it impossible for them to swim or breathe. It can cover their feeding grounds or be mistaken for food and end up in their bodies.

Chemicals can change the water and make it poisonous for marine life.

Time it takes to break down

plastic
400 years

aluminum
200 years

Styrofoam
80 years

foam
50 years

newspaper
6 weeks

cardboard
2 weeks

Tiza Mafira

Tiza Mafira is a lawyer and director of the Indonesia Plastic Bag Diet Movement. This group has campaigned to ban single-use plastic bags in the country. Her organization launched a petition in 2015 asking retailers to no longer give out plastic bags for free. The following year, a nationwide trial of a plastic bag charge was introduced. After six months, there had been a 55 percent reduction in the use of plastic bags. Several provinces began to prepare their own regulations and two cities in Indonesia have banned plastic bags in modern retail stores.

A Human Problem

There are many causes of pollution but almost all of them are human made. By not disposing of our garbage responsibly, it ends up in the ocean. Chemicals enter the water from factories or farmland. Ship traffic on the water creates engine noise.

Our oceans are not separate. They are joined into one World Ocean. The problems of one part spread to the others. Pollution can end up even in the remotest parts of the planet.

TACKLING THE PROBLEM

Although ocean pollution is a huge problem, people are working worldwide to solve it. Some efforts are local and focus on small-scale projects. Others are international groups that use their resources to tackle global ocean pollution.

Surfrider Vancouver Island is a local environmental group that works to preserve the waters around Vancouver Island in British Columbia, Canada. It organizes events such as monthly beach clean-ups. Other groups are international. They try to fight the problems of ocean pollution in cooperation with other countries. The United Nations Environment Programme (UNEP) group works to solve problems such as plastic pollution on a global scale. The United Nations' #BeatPlasticPollution campaign works to educate people on the dangers of too much plastic.

Organizations work to teach people how to create less pollution, such as shopping local and using reusable bags.

Project AWARE Foundation

The Project AWARE Foundation works with scuba divers across the globe to protect underwater environments. They focus on shark conservation and marine **debris**. If you want to take part in one of the organization's campaigns, you can explore the current Action Map to find the upcoming events or even start your own event. You can also adopt a dive site to help with the protection and monitoring of a particular area.

Top three items collected in beach clean-ups in 2019

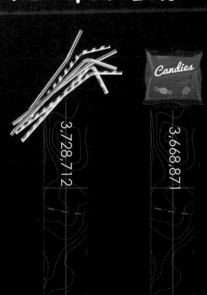

5,716,331

3,728,712

3,668,871

A Difficult Goal

Large- and small-scale projects face difficulties in ridding our oceans of pollution. Small-scale projects can make a difference in one area. But our oceans are all connected, so pollution and garbage travel. Groups doing beach clean-ups have to schedule them over and over as more waste from the oceans washes up on shore. International projects face problems in getting full cooperation from different countries. These countries may have different budgets for ocean conservation. Sometimes, they might be fighting politically and don't want to work together to reduce ocean pollution.

VISIBLE POLLUTION

Plastic waste is certainly the most visible type of pollution. We have all seen images of plastic water bottles, detergent bottles, plastic bags, and even plastic shoes floating on the water or washing up on beaches.

Plastic reaches the ocean in different ways. Sometimes, it is dumped directly into the ocean off ships or from shore. Other times, it is dumped into rivers and flows down to the sea. Wind can also pick up loose plastic, such as lightweight plastic bags, and blow them into rivers or the sea. Most of the plastic that ends up in the ocean is single-use plastic. These items are meant to be used only once, then thrown away. For example, plastic water bottles, plastic forks, and plastic straws are single-use plastics. If the plastic sinks to the sea floor, it covers feeding grounds, coral reefs, and breeding grounds.

Plastic can get tangled in boat propellers, fishing nets, and among **mangrove** trees (right).

Dumped fishing gear also makes up a large portion of ocean pollution.

of plastic pollution in oceans comes from single-use plastics.

Pollution Solution

Some communities are using huge nets to catch plastic and trash before it reaches the ocean. The city of Kwinana in Australia has installed nets over its storm sewers. They collected more than 816 pounds (370 kg) of waste in just a few months. Once this waste is collected, it is sorted. Natural material such as sticks and leaves are composted. The rest is either recycled or sent to landfills.

DAMAGE FROM MICROPLASTICS

What happens when plastic gets into the ocean? It does not break down into harmless natural elements. Instead, it breaks into smaller pieces called microplastic. When there is a lot of microplastic in the ocean, it becomes a toxic, plastic soup.

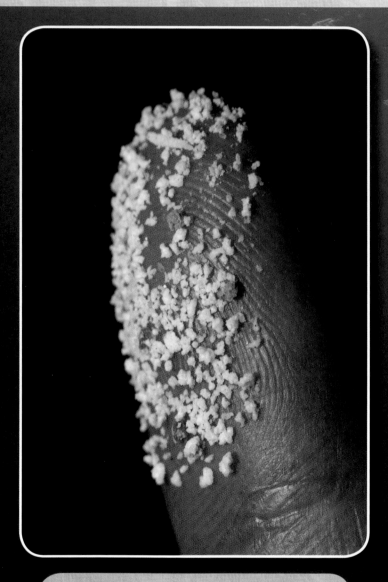

Microplastics are tiny—measuring 0.2 inches (5 mm) or less. Their size means they can pass through water filters.

Microplastics can stick to the **gills** of fish and other marine creatures, making it hard for them to breathe. Sea creatures can also **ingest** them while taking in water when they feed. Once inside their bodies, microplastics can poison them. Researchers at the University of Belgium say that people who eat shellfish may be eating up to 11,000 plastic particles in their food each year. At Plymouth University, scientists found plastic in one-third of fish caught for markets. Some stores are looking at having sections they can label as "plastic free" seafood.

Top Sources of ocean microplastics

clothing

tires

factory pellets

Microplastic Management

Microplastics are difficult to get out of the oceans. The pieces are so small that they are hard to see. They also slip through nets intended to scoop them up. Researchers are trying to remove plastic before it gets into our seafood. A teen from Ireland, Fionn Ferreira, developed a way to remove microplastics from the ocean as part of his entry for the Google Science Fair. His system uses oil to trap microplastics. Then the mixture is extracted from the water using a magnet.

PILES OF PLASTIC

Plastic is light, so it floats for a long time. Plastics are carried by waves farther and farther until currents **start to move them. Currents flow in circular patterns called gyres. These circular currents push plastics into large floating piles.**

Right now, there are five major gyres in our oceans. Once plastic enters a gyre, it almost never leaves. Gyres contain all sizes of plastic, from large containers or bags to microplastics. Cleaning up ocean plastic is extremely difficult. The ocean is huge. Even in a gyre, large and small plastic, can be spread far apart. It also sinks down through all layers of the ocean—it doesn't stay at the surface.

Size of the Great Pacific Garbage Patch

United States of America

San Franscisco

Mexico

Hawaii

The Great Pacific Garbage Patch is the largest accumulation of plastic and other debris in the oceans.

An Almost Impossible Task

Few people have come up with ideas on how to tackle the problem of plastic pollution far out in the oceans. Most organizations are focusing on beach clean-ups and preventing plastic from entering the ocean. One organization, The Ocean Cleanup, is trying to actively remove plastic from the gyres.

OCEAN ACTION

Boyan Slat, The Ocean Cleanup

The Ocean Cleanup was founded by Boyan Slat, who was only 18 at the time! In 2013, Boyan came up with an idea that would help remove plastics and other garbage from the oceans quickly, and for less money than it usually costs. Today, his idea has grown into a real organization. It has performed a lot of research and tests. Early system problems have led to delays and redesign, but in the fall of 2019, the project began catching ocean plastic. His idea includes a floating system that gathers ocean plastic at sea. He also created solar-powered boats, called Interceptors, that collect plastic in rivers before it reaches the ocean.

Boyan Slat on the Interceptor 002 in Klang River, Malaysia

THREATS TO OCEAN LIFE

Plastics, especially microplastics, do not float on the surface forever. Over time, waves and wind cause them to sink down until they settle on the ocean floor.

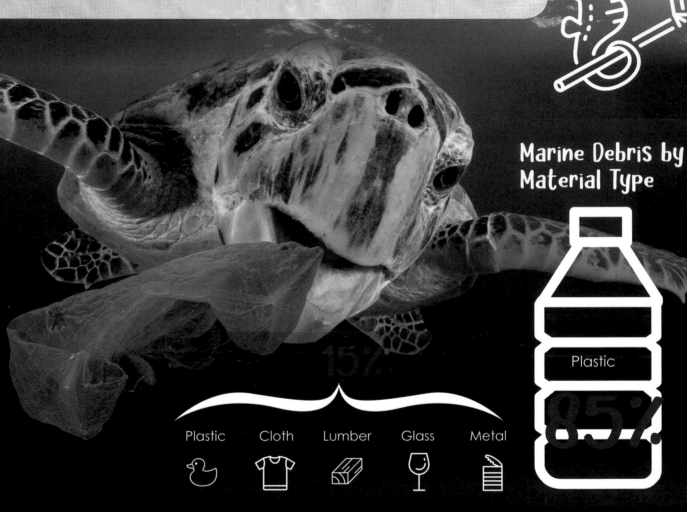

Marine Debris by Material Type

Plastic — 15%

Plastic   Cloth   Lumber   Glass   Metal

Plastic — 85%

While floating down, plastics cause problems for marine creatures. Plastic bags can look like food to fish or turtles. Plastic rings to hold bottles or cans can tangle or trap an animal's fins, legs, or head. This can restrict their movement and cause them to starve or drown. But when these large or small pieces settle on the sea floor, they cause more problems.

All of the effects of microplastics on the ocean floor damages marine creatures' abilities to reproduce and grow.

Plastics on the Ocean Floor

On the ocean floor, plastics cover feeding and **spawning** grounds. They also have an impact on habitats and make it difficult for creatures to hide from **predators**. Once on the sea floor, microplastics mix with sand or **sediment**. There, they can slowly release toxic chemicals and change the way plants and non-moving creatures such as corals attach to surfaces. Studies also show that mussels have trouble attaching to rocks after ingesting microplastics.

Removing microplastics from sediment is difficult. Researchers at the Plymouth Marine Laboratory in the United Kingdom have worked on a solution. They know that different particles float at different levels in different liquids. They use that fact to separate **microplastics** from sand in a special chamber. To slow the amount of microplastics in oceans, many countries are also banning microbeads which are found in certain products.

mussels

SPRAWLING SPILLS

A major source of ocean pollution is from oil and gas spills. There are more than 50,000 ships, boats, and platforms for drilling for oil on the oceans at any one time. There are thousands of oil spills each year.

1990's	2000's	2010's
1,249,000 tons	229,000 tons	180,800 tons
(1,133,000 metric tons)	(208,000 metric tons)	(164,000 metric tons)

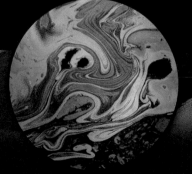

The amount of oil spilled into the ocean each year has decreased.

Some spills leak about a barrel full of oil in the ocean, while others spill more than 10,000 barrels worth. **Oil slicks** spread with ocean waves and currents. The oil can **suffocate** fish. It also covers the feathers of sea birds so they cannot fly or keep warm.

Oil on the surface of the water can block sunlight. This makes it impossible for ocean plants to convert sunlight into food, energy, and oxygen. This can affect how much oxygen is in our atmosphere.

Maurice the Whale

Soo Bin Cho, Cheyenne Bridge, Sage Nelson, and Lauren Richardson are a group of students who wanted to show others how litter has a direct impact on marine wildlife. They created "Maurice," a whale mural painted on a wooden board with a garbage bag for a stomach. They brought Maurice to a local pier. There they encouraged visitors to pick up trash and deposit it in Maurice's "stomach."

Quick Cleanups

Oil slicks on the surface of the water can be contained inside floating barriers called booms. The oil is then sucked up with skimmer machines. Some of the oil can even be reused. But once an oil slick is broken up by waves and wind, skimming isn't effective. Scientists are developing new foams to soak up oil. They are also testing a system of **buoys** that can detect oil in their area and transmit information quickly. The quicker a spill is detected, the better it can be cleaned up.

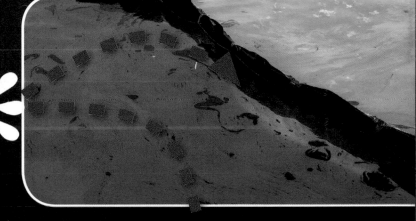

MARINE MINING

Metals like aluminum, copper, nickel, zinc, silver, and gold are used for everything from jewelry to computers. Demand for these metals is rising. Many sites on land have none left. Mining companies are looking to the ocean floor as a source for these metals.

Right now, companies are mostly investigating to see if it is possible to make money mining under the ocean. But mining the ocean floor creates many problems. Machines scrape the ocean floor, which destroys habitats. Also, this kicks up sediment that can block sunlight, suffocate creatures, or harm **filter feeders**, such as clams. Another problem is that many deep ocean organisms such as coral reefs grow slowly and only reproduce late in life. This means that if they are damaged, they won't recover quickly or maybe not at all. Mining also creates waste products such as mercury.

Mercury builds up in fish and then is ingested by people when eating seafood. Too much causes health issues.

Damaged coral reef •••••••••••••••••• Five years

It takes a coral reef five to 10 years to recover from damage.

The National Oceanic and Atmospheric Administration (NOAA) in the United States. also conducts underwater searches to learn more about the ocean floor and the ecosystems there. They use remotely operated vehicles (ROVs) (above) to gather data and take samples.

Ten Years

Seeking Safe Mining

We know so little about the deep ocean that no one is certain what the short- and long-term effects of ocean floor mining will be. Researchers are doing studies to understand more about the species that live deep in the ocean. They are working with an international team of scientists called the Deep Ocean Stewardship Initiative. They are helping to figure out the dangers of underwater mining, and how to avoid polluting the ocean. Recent studies have shown that **ecosystems** on the seabed of the Pacific Ocean have not fully recovered from experimental mining tested nearly 30 years ago.

NOISE POLLUTION

In the darkness of the deep oceans, many creatures do not use sight to find their way or find their food. They use other senses: touch, smell, and hearing. Sound travels faster and often farther in water than through air. Noise caused by human activity threatens creatures that depend on their sense of sound.

Loud noises can damage the sensitive hearing of some creatures. It can disrupt migration patterns. It makes finding food and members of a family group more difficult. Noise pollution also raises stress levels. Large ships, **sonar**, ocean floor mining, and explosion testing all contribute to underwater noise.

Vessel noise affects a marine animal's ability to:...

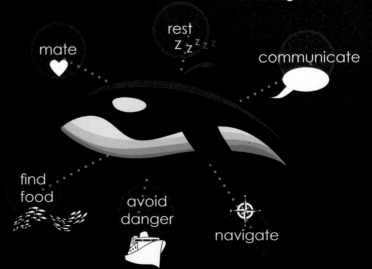

mate

rest z z z z z

communicate

find food

avoid danger

navigate

Dolphins rely on their sense of sound to communicate in groups called pods.

Oceana

Oceana is the largest organization in the world solely devoted to marine conservation. It was established in 2001 by The Pew Charitable Trusts, the Oak Foundation, Marisla Foundation, Sandler Foundation, and Rockefeller Brothers Fund. Oceana is involved in efforts to end major sources of ocean pollution such as plastics, oil, mercury, aquaculture or seafood farming, and shipping emissions. Oceana was successful in New York in helping to create a ban on foam food containers and foam packing peanuts.

Sound Solutions

Acoustic Integration Models (AIMs) help scientists measure underwater noise. By measuring the levels of sound, they help us to understand how noise pollution affects marine animals. AIMs are often used near shipping lanes or near offshore wind turbines. The AIM system found that the speed of cruise ships affects how damaging noises are. By slowing the speed of ships, the sound is not as disruptive to marine creatures. It also found that stopping traffic at certain times of the day gives creatures a break from noise, helping them communicate and reorient themselves.

DOWN THE DRAIN

Sewage is wastewater from homes, ships, and buildings. This includes what we flush out of bathrooms. When untreated sewage is dumped directly into oceans, or rivers leading to oceans, it causes problems.

Direct dumping releases diseases and **parasites** directly into the water. Industrial waste from factories and processing plants is sometimes dumped directly into our waterways, too. The waste can include acids, scrap metals, sludge, and coal ash. Bacteria in the water use oxygen to break down all kinds of waste. This can lead to them using up the oxygen that is needed by other marine creatures to breathe.

In 1972, countries around the world got together in London, England, to create rules about dumping waste in the sea. The regulations are called the London Convention. Under these rules, chemicals, **radioactive** waste, and untreated sewage is banned. However countries that do not have good waste management are still dumping banned items into our oceans. The London Convention is working with these countries to develop strategies to avoid illegal dumping.

The many ways to reduce wastewater at home include fixing leaky pipes and using water-saving appliances.

Only 10% of medicine is absorbed in the body.

The rest is expelled as waste.

80%

of all bodies of water contain pharmaceuticals.

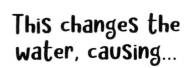

This changes the water, causing...

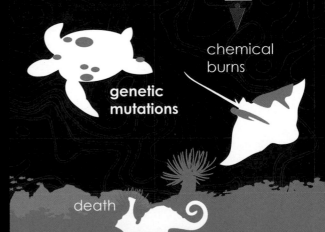

genetic mutations

chemical burns

death

Creating Cleaner Water

Sometimes waste in waterways is not on purpose. Storms and blockages can cause sewers to back up or overflow. Some cities such as Toronto, Ontario, are building overflow pipes to store extra wastewater during storms. Some cruise ships now have water treatment plants onboard. They use **bioreactors** in which bacteria breaks down human waste and food scraps. The liquid is treated with **UV radiation** instead of chemicals. Then, the clean water is discharged back into the sea.

RUNOFF RISKS

Ocean pollution also comes from farm and fish farm fertilizer runoff. Fertilizers give the plants or marine organisms what they need to grow and produce the food we eat. But when it accidentally makes its way into waterways or outside fish farms, it can wash out to the oceans.

Many farmers and fish farmers add fertilizers to their fields and water systems in the form of chemical fertilizers and animal manure. But if the plants or animals do not use up the fertilizer, it can wash off the land with heavy rain or flow back into waterways and wash out to the oceans. This causes algae blooms when algae get more **nutrients** than normal. Algae blooms can use up all the oxygen in the water, suffocating fish. Algae blooms can also give off toxins to poison plant and animal life.

An algae bloom completely covers this beach in China, which meets the Yellow Sea.

Algae blooms mostly cause fishing and tourism industries to lose money. They kill fish and make beaches unusable.

Cost of algae blooms in United States

lakes

$2 billion

coasts

$82 million

Attacking Algae

We have different methods of dealing with algae blooms. Sometimes they are treated with chemicals, but the chemicals used may also be harmful to the ocean environment. Other methods include adding oxygen or mixing the water. Both are slow processes to get rid of excess algae. New technology involves using **ultrasound waves**. These makes algae sink to where it has no sunlight to grow and feed. The benefit is that this method is harmless to fish and plants. The problem with this method is that it is difficult to cover a large area. It can also be an expensive, and lengthy process.

GET INVOLVED

Reducing pollution in our oceans is everyone's responsibility. Changes in our own daily lives can affect the amount of waste or toxins that find their way to the oceans.

Plastic waste flows or gets blown out to sea from land. By reducing how much plastic we buy, use, and throw away we can cut down the amount of plastic that ends up in the oceans. We can all look for alternatives to plastic, especially single-use plastic. We can choose to use paper plates instead of Styrofoam, reusable beeswax covers instead of plastic cling wrap, paper straws instead of plastic, and even bamboo toothbrushes.

The United Nations (UN) focuses on preserving oceans as part of its Sustainable Development Goals. Goal 14 is called Life Below Water. The UN looks to youth to get involved in creating a sustainable world.

14 LIFE BELOW WATER

Collaborate!

World Oceans Day, on June 8 each year, is a good time to remind ourselves of the importance of keeping our oceans clean. It is a good time to join in activities and projects such as local beach clean-ups. It is a day to remember that our oceans give us a food supply, oxygen in our atmosphere, **moderate** our climate, and allow us to travel the world. Picking vacations with the least impact on ocean animals and habitats is a good choice we can make.

We can support organizations that work to create laws to reduce noise pollution or regulate ocean mining. Using less fertilizer on our gardens, and searching for local produce that also uses less, helps prevent runoff into our waterways. Cutting down on our use of fossil fuels by riding a bike rather than getting a ride in a car will slow climate change. Even small changes can add up and help keep our oceans healthy.

GLOSSARY

bioreactors Machines that use living organisms to break down substances

buoys Floating objects anchored to the ocean floor

commercial Relating to buying and selling; profit making

currents Water moving in a specific direction, usually through a larger body of water

debris Scattered pieces of waste

ecosystem A community of living things and their environment

filter feeders Marine creatures that strain tiny organisms out of the water

genetic mutations Changes in the genes that make up a living thing

gills The organs on the sides of fish through which they breathe

ingest Take food or drink into the body

mangrove A tree that grows in coastal swamps

microbeads Tiny plastic particles added to cosmetics and other products to help clean things such as skin and teeth

moderate Make less extreme

nutrients Substances that help living things survive and grow

oil slicks Layers of oil floating on a large surface of ocean

parasites Organisms that live in or on other organisms

predators Animals that hunt and kill other animals for food

preserve Keep in its original condition

radioactive Having a dangerous form of energy called radiation

resources Supplies such as money that allow people or organizations to complete tasks

sediment Tiny pieces of silt, sand, or rocks

sonar Using sound waves to find objects underwater

spawning The process of releasing eggs and sperm to reproduce

suffocate Cause to die from lack of oxygen

toxic Poisonous

ultrasound waves Sound waves that humans cannot hear

UV radiation Invisible rays of radiation that come from the Sun

LEARNING MORE

Books

Eriksson, Ann. *Dive In!: Exploring Our Connection with the Ocean*. Orca Book Publishers, 2018.

Howell, Izzi. *Pollution Eco Facts*. Crabtree Publishing Company, 2020.

Jakubiak, David J. *What Can We Do About Oil Spills and Ocean Pollution?* PowerKids Press, 2011.

Websites

https://bit.ly/2V51mxd
National Geographic Kids investigates plastic pollution and our oceans.

https://ocean.si.edu/conservation/pollution
The Smithsonian Institute's Ocean Portal has articles on all types of ocean pollution.

http://www.kidsagainstplastic.co.uk/tag/gyre
Kids Against Plastic is a website with articles and videos about plastic pollution, including the plastic gyres in the oceans.

INDEX

ABOUT THE AUTHOR

Natalie Hyde has written more than 90 fiction and non-fiction books for young readers. When she gets time to relax, one of her favorite places to be is beside the ocean on a warm, sandy beach.